# Market Research Math for Small Business

*A Practical Guide to the Math You Need for Understanding Your Business' Customers and Competition*

Steven A. Wright, MBA PhD JD

**Copyright © 2024** - *Macadamia Solutions LLC*. All rights reserved. The content contained within this book may not be reproduced, duplicated, or transmitted without direct written permission from the author or the publisher, except in the case of brief quotations embodied in critical reviews and certain other noncommercial uses permitted by copyright law. Under no circumstances will any blame or legal liability be held against the publisher or author for any damages, compensation, or monetary loss due to the information contained within this book, either directly or indirectly. You are responsible for your own choices, actions, and results.

**Legal Notice:** This book is copyright-protected. This book is for personal use only. You may not amend, distribute, sell, use, quote, or paraphrase any part or the content within this book without the consent of the author or publisher, except in the case of brief quotations embodied in critical reviews and certain other noncommercial uses permitted by copyright law.

**Disclaimer Notice:** Please note that the information contained within this document is for informational, educational, and entertainment purposes only. All efforts have been made to present accurate, up-to-date, and reliable, complete information. No warranties of any kind are declared or implied. *Readers acknowledge that the author is not engaged in the rendering of legal, financial, medical, or professional advice.* The content within this book has been derived from various sources. Please consult a licensed professional before attempting any techniques outlined in this book. Designations used by companies to distinguish their products are often claimed as trademarks. *All brand names and product names used in this book and on its cover are trade names, service marks, trademarks, and registered trademarks of their respective owners.* The publishers and the book author are not associated with any product or vendor mentioned in this book. None of the companies referenced within the book have endorsed the book. By reading this document, the reader agrees that under no circumstances shall the author be liable for any loss, direct or indirect, which is incurred as a result of the use of the information contained within this document, including, but not limited to, errors, omissions, or inaccuracies.

# Table of Contents

**CHAPTER 1: INTRODUCTION TO MARKET RESEARCH ..................................................1**
    UNDERSTANDING THE IMPORTANCE OF MARKET RESEARCH ........................................................1
    SETTING RESEARCH GOALS AND OBJECTIVES: YOUR ROADMAP TO SUCCESS ...........................2
    YOUR TOOLKIT FOR UNDERSTANDING DATA: BASIC STATISTICAL CONCEPTS: .........................4
    YOUR COMMAND CENTER FOR MARKET INSIGHTS: SETTING UP YOUR RESEARCH ENVIRONMENT ........................................................................................................................................7
    ONLINE RESOURCES: YOUR RESEARCH GOLDMINE ...............................................................9

**CHAPTER 2: FINDING, COLLECTING, AND ANALYZING ONLINE DATA ...............11**
    SECONDARY DATA SOURCES: YOUR TREASURE TROVE OF INFORMATION .................................12
    CREATING A PRIMARY DATA COLLECTION PLAN: YOUR ROADMAP TO SUCCESS ........................16
    SURVEYS AND ONLINE POLLS: YOUR DIRECT LINE TO CUSTOMER INSIGHTS .........................18

**CHAPTER 3: WORKING WITH STATISTICAL FUNCTIONS IN SPREADSHEETS ...22**
    MARKET RESEARCH PROBLEMS CRYING OUT FOR VISUALIZATION ..........................................22
    DESCRIPTIVE STATISTICS .................................................................................................24
    INFERENTIAL STATISTICS AND HYPOTHESIS TESTING ...........................................................28
    CORRELATION AND REGRESSION ANALYSIS ........................................................................35
    SUPERCHARGING YOUR MARKET RESEARCH: HEURISTICS & AI PREDICTIVE TECHNIQUES: ......39

**CHAPTER 4: APPLYING MARKET RESEARCH INSIGHTS TO GROW YOUR BUSINESS ....................................................................................................................42**
    IDENTIFYING MARKET OPPORTUNITIES AND TRENDS: YOUR ROADMAP TO SUCCESS ..............42
    DEVELOPING A MARKETING MIX AND TACTICS: YOUR RECIPE FOR SUCCESS ..........................44

**CONCLUSION: YOUR JOURNEY THROUGH MARKET RESEARCH MATH ...........47**

**GLOSSARY........................................................................................................................48**

**RESOURCES .....................................................................................................................52**
    MARKETING .....................................................................................................................52
    VISUALIZATION ................................................................................................................52
    STATISTICS ......................................................................................................................52
    SURVEYS .........................................................................................................................52
    GOOGLE APPS .................................................................................................................53

# Chapter 1: Introduction to Market Research

Don't worry if math isn't your favorite subject in school; we're going to make this journey fun, accessible, and incredibly valuable for your business. If you're a small business owner or entrepreneur, with this book, you've just taken a crucial step towards understanding your market better.

## Understanding the Importance of Market Research

Imagine you're about to open a new coffee shop. You've got the perfect location in mind. Your favorite barista lined up. You're ready to pour your soul (and coffee) into this venture. But wait - how do you know if there's a demand for another coffee shop in the area? What if the locals prefer tea? This is where market research comes in, and it's not just for big corporations with deep pockets.

Market research is the process of gathering, analyzing, and interpreting information about your market, including your potential customers and competitors. It's like having a friendly conversation with your potential customers (before you even open your doors). This information becomes the foundation for making intelligent, informed business decisions.

### The Power of Statistics in Market Research

Now, you might be wondering, "I thought you were talking with customers; where does math fit into all this?" Statistics are the secret sauce that turns raw data into actionable insights. Describing all the information you gather with statistics allows you to spot trends, understand preferences, and predict future behavior.

For example, instead of just guessing that "lots of people" in your area drink coffee, statistics can tell you, for example, that 68% of adults in your town consume coffee daily. That's a much more reliable basis for decision-making!

## Common Pitfalls to Avoid

While market research is incredibly powerful, it has its pitfalls. One common mistake is relying too heavily on secondary research (information that already exists) without conducting any primary research (information you gather firsthand). Another is falling into the confirmation bias trap - only looking for data that supports what you already believe. Remember, the goal of market research is to uncover the truth about your market, not to confirm your existing ideas. Keep an open mind, and be prepared for surprises!

## Types of Market Research Methods

Market research comes in many flavors, and understanding the different types can help you choose the right approach for your needs: **Primary vs. Secondary Research:** Primary research collects new data specifically for your project, while secondary research uses existing data from other sources. **Qualitative vs. Quantitative Research:** Qualitative research explores the "why" behind behaviors and preferences, often through interviews or focus groups. Quantitative research deals with numbers and statistics, typically through surveys or data analysis. **Online vs. Offline Research:** Online research methods like social media analysis and online surveys are increasingly popular. However, for some businesses, traditional offline methods like in-person interviews or mail surveys may be easier.

As we dive deeper into this book, we'll explore these methods and the math behind them in more detail. Don't worry - before you know it, you'll be crunching numbers like a pro! Market research isn't about getting a perfect prediction of the future. It's about reducing uncertainty in order to make more informed decisions. Read on to discover how a little bit of math can make a big difference in your business success!

# Setting Research Goals and Objectives: Your Roadmap to Success

Let's begin by setting research goals and objectives! Think of this as creating a roadmap for your market research journey. Without a clear destination in mind, you might end up taking some scenic detours that, while interesting, don't get you where you need to go. So, let's make sure we're pointing your research in the right direction!

## Defining Research Questions and Hypotheses: What Do You Really Want to Know?

Imagine you're at a coffee shop (yes, we're sticking with our coffee shop example - I must be craving a latte!). You're chatting with a friend about your business idea, and they start peppering you with questions. "Who's going to buy your coffee?" "What will make your shop different?" "How much are people willing to pay for a cup of joe?"

These are precisely the kinds of questions you need to be asking in your market research. Your research questions are the big, overarching queries you want to answer. They might look something like this:

- What is the demand for specialty coffee in our town?
- Who are our potential customers, and what are their coffee preferences?
- How much are people willing to pay for a premium cup of coffee?

Now, your hypotheses are your educated guesses about the answers to these questions. For example:

- We believe that at least 30% of adults in our town would be interested in specialty coffee.
- Our target customers are likely to be young professionals aged 25-40.
- Customers would be willing to pay up to $5 for a premium cup of coffee.

Don't worry if your guesses are wrong - that's the whole point of doing the research!

## Identifying Target Audiences and Markets: Who Are We Talking To?

Now that we know what we want to find out, we need to figure out who we will ask. This is where identifying your target audience comes in. Your target audience is the group of people most likely to be interested in your product or service. For our coffee shop, we might decide to focus on:

- Local residents within a 5-mile radius
- Office workers in nearby business districts
- College students from the local university

Remember, you can't be all things to all people. By clearly defining your target customers, you can tailor your research (and eventually your marketing) to speak directly to the people most likely to become your customers.

## Budgeting for Market Research: Making Every Dollar Count

I know what you're thinking - "Great, another expense for my new business!" But here's the thing: market research doesn't have to break the bank. In fact, investing in research now can save you a lot of money (and headaches) later. When budgeting for market research, consider the following:

**DIY vs. Professional:** Many aspects of market research can be done yourself, especially with online tools. But for more complex studies, you should budget for professional help.

**Time vs. Money:** Remember, your time is valuable too. Sometimes, it's worth spending a bit more money to save a lot of time.

**Free Resources:** Remember free resources like public libraries, government databases, and online forums.

**Start Small:** You don't need to do everything at once. Start with the most critical questions and expand your research as your business grows.

A good rule of thumb is to allocate about 2-5% of your projected first-year revenue to market research. Don't let that number scare you - even a tiny budget can yield valuable insights. Remember, the goal is to gather enough information to make informed decisions. It's about finding that sweet spot where you're confident in your understanding of the market without overextending your resources.

So, are you ready to set some goals and start exploring your market? Great! In the following sections, we'll dive into the nitty-gritty of how to actually conduct your research and make sense of all that data.

# Your Toolkit for Understanding Data: Basic Statistical Concepts:

Alright, folks, it's time to open up our statistical toolbox! Don't worry if the word "statistics" makes you break out in a cold sweat - we're going to keep things simple, practical, and, dare I say, even fun.

But first - what even is a statistic? A statistic, in its simplest form, is a numerical value derived from a set of data that summarizes or describes the characteristics of that data. More specifically, it is any quantity computed from values in a sample that serves a statistical purpose, such as estimating a population parameter, describing a sample, or testing a hypothesis. Think of statistics as the secret decoder ring for all the information you'll gather in your market research. Let's dive in!

## Descriptive Statistics: Painting a Picture with Numbers

First up, we have descriptive statistics. These are like the Cliffs Notes of your data - they give you a quick summary of what's going on. Descriptive statistics help you organize, summarize, and present your data in a way that's easy to understand.

Some standard descriptive statistics include:

**Mean:** The average of all your numbers.
**Median:** The middle number when your data is ordered from lowest to highest.
**Mode:** The number that appears most often in your data set.
**Range:** The difference between the highest and lowest numbers.

Pros of descriptive statistics: They're easy to calculate and understand. They give you a quick snapshot of your data. They're great for summarizing large amounts of information.

Cons of descriptive statistics: They don't tell the whole story - essential details might be hidden. They can be misleading if your data has extreme values (outliers).

## Inferential Statistics: Crystal Ball Gazing (Sort of)

Now, let's talk about inferential statistics. If descriptive statistics are about summarizing what you have, inferential statistics are about making educated guesses (predictions) about what you don't have. They help you draw conclusions about a larger population based on a smaller sample. For example, you might use inferential statistics to estimate how many people in your entire town would be interested in your coffee shop based on a survey of 100 people.

Inferential statistics allow you to make predictions and test hypotheses. They help you make decisions with incomplete information. They're crucial for understanding if your results are statistically significant. Inferential statistics are more complex than descriptive statistics and can be intimidating for beginners. There's always a margin of error - they're not 100% accurate. They require careful sampling to be reliable. The key difference? Descriptive statistics describe what is, while inferential statistics predict what might be.

## Non-Statistical Shortcuts of Decision Making: Heuristics and AI

Last but not least, let's talk about heuristics. For the mathematical purist, these are not statistics. These are mental shortcuts or "rules of thumb" that help us make quick decisions without having to crunch numbers. Heuristics are problem-solving techniques that rely on practical experience and common sense rather than precise rules. AI tools are a form of heuristics because they provide quick, efficient solutions to complex problems, much like mental shortcuts. AI systems use patterns and generalizations to navigate through vast amounts of data and identify relevant information effectively.

Heuristics and AI tools are quick and easy to use. They can be surprisingly accurate in many situations and don't require complex calculations. Heuristics and AI tools can also be subject to inherent biases and errors. They might oversimplify complex situations. They are not always based on solid evidence.

There are additional risks of using AI as a heuristic tool. The "black box" nature of some AI algorithms does not follow decision logic - they just detect patterns, potentially leading to unintended consequences. AI tools may generate plausible-sounding but incorrect information, known as "AI hallucinations," which can be difficult to detect and verify. Software tools like AI rely on patterns detected from large data sets. This can be great for automating the recognition of established patterns to trigger existing business processes. Without appropriate human guidance, it does not necessarily provide the critical thinking skills and business acumen required to correctly identify new business opportunities. AI models may perpetuate biases present in their training data. This could lead your business to unfair or discriminatory outcomes for your customers. You cannot simply delegate commercial responsibility (or potential liability) to AI software.

While heuristics and AI tools can be valuable for quick decision-making and problem-solving, it's crucial to balance their use with critical thinking and awareness of their limitations. Understanding the potential risks associated with AI-powered heuristics is essential to mitigate potential negative outcomes.

# Your Command Center for Market Insights: Setting Up Your Research Environment

Think of this as creating your small business command center for market insights. Just like a chef needs a well-organized kitchen to whip up culinary masterpieces, you need a well-structured research environment to cook up brilliant market strategies. Let's dive in and see how we can make this happen! For this book, we'll construct your command center for market insights using freely available Google tools. This has the additional advantage that there are many excellent tutorials available online to walk you through how to effectively utilize these tools. For those of you who are digital nomads, these Google tools are available online where you have adequate Internet access.

## Why Establishing a Research Environment Matters

A dedicated research environment is needed to support the ongoing cycle of market research and business decision-making. This cycle typically follows these steps: **Define** research questions, **Collect** market data, **Analyze** market data, Make business **Decisions**, **and Repeat,** monitoring your business as the market changes. A good research environment helps you manage this process efficiently. Carefully structuring your research environment enables you to automate tasks where necessary.

## Google *Sheets*: Your Data Powerhouse

Google Sheets is the cornerstone of your research environment. It allows you to store and organize your data, perform calculations and statistical analyses, Create charts and visualizations, and collaborate with team members in real-time.

## Google *Docs*: Your Report Hub

Google Docs seamlessly integrates with Sheets, enabling you to create dynamic reports that automatically update with your latest data, embed charts and tables directly from Sheets, and collaborate on market research findings and analysis.

## Linking Sheets and Docs

To insert data from Sheets into Docs:
1. Open both the Sheet and Doc
2. Copy the desired cells from Sheets
3. Paste into Docs, selecting "Link to spreadsheet."

The data will appear with the original formatting intact and will update automatically when the source Sheet changes

## Google *Forms*: Data Collection Made Easy

Use Google Forms to create surveys and questionnaires, automatically populate Sheets with responses, and analyze results directly in Sheets.

## Google *Drive*: Organize Your Research

Utilize Google Drive to store and organize all your research documents. For example, if you are researching multiple markets, keep the files associated with analyzing those markets in separate folders. It can also keep the data in separate Google Sheets files from the analysis tools. Once the data has been imported, consider protecting ranges or sheets to protect them from being overwritten. The analysis tools that you develop for your business should be similarly safeguarded (once you are happy with them) to prevent accidental modifications. You can share folders with team members and access your research from any device. In doing so, you should also consider using the available sharing permissions to protect your hard work here. This data repository for your small business contains essential market and competitive insights, as well as business plans. You should give some consideration to your business' needs for securing this data.

By leveraging these interconnected Google tools, you can create a robust, automated research environment without the need for external applications. This ecosystem supports the ongoing cycle of defining research questions, collecting data, analyzing results, and making informed business decisions.

# Online Resources: Your Research Goldmine

The internet is a treasure trove of market research resources. Here are some types of online resources you'll find invaluable:
- Government databases (e.g., census data, economic indicators)
- Industry reports and whitepapers
- Social media analytics tools
- Online survey platforms
- Competitor websites and annual reports

These resources can help you at various stages of your research process, from defining questions to collecting and analyzing data.

## AI in Market Research: Your Digital Research Assistant

Artificial Intelligence is revolutionizing market research, and it's not just for big corporations anymore. AI tools can help small businesses throughout the research cycle:

Define research questions by identifying trends and patterns in existing data

Collect data by automating web scraping or survey distribution

Analyze large datasets quickly and identify patterns that humans might miss

Generate insights to inform business decisions

Monitor ongoing performance by continuously analyzing incoming data

Be active and assume that software can create a new business for you! While AI tools can be potent, it's important to remember that they're not infallible. Always combine AI insights with your own critical thinking and industry knowledge.

## The Ongoing Research Cycle

Remember, market research isn't a one-and-done activity. It's an ongoing process that should be integrated into your business operations. Here's how you might structure this ongoing cycle:

**Define Research Questions:** What do you need to know about your market or customers?

**Collect Data:** Use surveys, analyze sales data, or gather information from online sources.

**Analyze Data:** Use your spreadsheet and AI tools to crunch the numbers and identify insights.

**Make Business Decisions:** Use your findings to inform your strategy and operations.

**Monitor and Repeat:** Continuously track critical metrics to stay up-to-date with market changes.

Setting up your research environment might seem like a lot of work upfront, but the cycle of research demonstrates the value. A well-organized research environment supports this ongoing cycle, helping you quickly make better decisions and continuously improve your business performance. So, roll up your sleeves, fire up that spreadsheet, and let's get researching!

# Chapter 2: Finding, Collecting, and Analyzing Online Data

Hey there, data enthusiast! Let's talk about one of the most common questions in market research: "How much data do I actually need?" It's like asking how much coffee you need to start your day - the answer is: it depends!

## The Goldilocks Zone of Data Collection

You want your market data to be just right - not too little, not too much. If there is too little data, your insights will not be reliable. Too much, and you could be drowning in numbers (and data collection costs) without gaining extra value. Let's break it down:

**Qualitative vs. Quantitative**: Sometimes, a few in-depth interviews can be more valuable than hundreds of survey responses. It's all about the type of insights you're after.

**Statistical Validity:** Decision tests associated with statistics are typically presented in the scientific literature with an associated confidence interval. Adequate sample size is needed to achieve an acceptable confidence interval. In most cases, you need to aim for at least 30 samples to generate statistically significant results. Statistical validity may be possible with fewer samples if the data follows a normal data distribution reasonably closely.

## The Hidden Costs of Data

Now, let's talk money. Data isn't free, even when it seems like it is. Here are some costs to keep in mind:

**Purchase/Access Costs:** Some data sources charge for access. These can range from a few bucks for a survey tool subscription to thousands for industry reports.

**Operational Costs:** This includes the time you spend collecting, storing, and analyzing data. Remember, your time is valuable too!

**Data Governance:** Once you have data, you need to manage it responsibly. This might mean investing in secure storage solutions or training staff on data handling.

**Regulatory Compliance:** Depending on your location and the type of data you're collecting, you might need to comply with privacy regulations like GDPR or CCPA. This can involve legal fees and potential fines if you mess up.

## Sampling from Large Data Sets: The Art of Picking the Right Slice

If you're lucky enough to have access to a large dataset, you might think, "Great! I'll just use all of it!" But hold your horses - sometimes, less is more. Here's why:

**Uniformity**: Is your data set consistent throughout? If not, you might need to stratify your sample to ensure you're getting a representative slice.

**Representativeness**: Make sure your sample reflects the diversity of your target population. If your coffee shop is in a college town, your sample should include a diverse mix of students, faculty, and locals.

**Sample Selection Process:** Random sampling is often your best bet for unbiased results. But sometimes, you might need to use stratified or cluster sampling to ensure you're capturing all important subgroups.

Remember, the goal isn't to collect ALL the data - it's to collect the RIGHT data. Think quality over quantity. A well-chosen sample of 500 can often tell you more than a poorly selected sample of 5,000. In the end, the amount of data you need for your market research depends on your specific research questions, budget, and resources. Start small, focus on quality, and scale up as needed.

Next, we'll dive into the nitty-gritty of finding and collecting this data online. Get ready to become a data detective!

# Secondary Data Sources: Your Treasure Trove of Information

Hey there, small business owner! Ready to dive into the world of secondary data? It's like finding a treasure chest full of valuable insights; the best part is someone else has already dug for you!

## Your Tax Dollars at Work: Government Reports

Market Research Math for Small Business

Remember all those taxes you pay? Well, here's where you get some return on investment! Government agencies are goldmines of data. The table below lists 10 government agencies that make data available. Depending on your industry, other regulatory agencies may also provide relevant data.

| Government Agency | Website URL | Description |
|---|---|---|
| U.S. Census Bureau | census.gov | Offers comprehensive demographic, economic, and geographic data about the U.S. population, including the Economic Census and American Community Survey. |
| Bureau of Labor Statistics (BLS) | bls.gov | Provides data on labor market activity, working conditions, price changes, and productivity in the U.S. economy, including employment statistics and wage data. |
| Federal Reserve Economic Data (FRED) | fred.stlouisfed.org | A comprehensive database of economic data, including interest rates, employment figures, and inflation metrics that are essential for market analysis. |
| Small Business Administration (SBA) | sba.gov | Offers resources and statistics specifically for small businesses, including market research tools and guides to understanding competitive landscapes. |

| | | |
|---|---|---|
| National Center for Education Statistics (NCES) | nces.ed.gov | Provides data on education in the U.S., including demographics and trends that can inform market research related to educational products and services. |
| U.S. Economic Research Service (ERS) | ers.usda.gov | Offers economic analysis and data pertaining to agriculture, food markets, and rural economies, useful for businesses in the food industry. |
| National Oceanic and Atmospheric Administration (NOAA) | noaa.gov | Provides climate and weather data that can be crucial for industries affected by environmental factors, such as agriculture and tourism. |
| U.S. Department of Commerce | commerce.gov | Offers a variety of economic data, including trade statistics and industry reports that can help businesses understand market conditions. |
| Centers for Disease Control and Prevention (CDC) | cdc.gov | Provides health-related statistics that can inform market research in healthcare products and services, as well as public health trends affecting consumer behavior. |
| National Institute of Standards and Technology (NIST) | nist.gov | Offers standards, guidelines, and statistical data relevant to various industries that can aid in product development and quality assurance efforts. |

# Industry Studies: Standing on the Shoulders of Giants

Industry associations and professional organizations often publish reports that can give you a bird's-eye view of your market:

**Trade publications** are like gossip magazines for your industry but with more graphs and fewer scandals.

**Market research reports**: Sometimes, you might need to shell out a few bucks, but these can be worth their weight in gold.

## Using Internet Search for Market Research: Become a Google Ninja

The internet is like an all-you-can-eat buffet of information. The trick is knowing how to fill your plate with the good stuff!

## Effective Search Techniques

Use quotation marks for exact phrases: "small business market research."

Minus sign to exclude terms: market research -big business

Site-specific searches: site:edu market research methods

## Evaluating Online Sources: Don't Believe Everything You Read

Not all that glitters is gold, especially on the internet. Here's how to spot the real deal: **Check the source:** Is it a reputable organization or just someone's blog? **Look for recent data:** In the fast-paced business world, last year's news is ancient history. **Cross-reference:** You're on the right track if multiple reliable sources say the same thing. In an era where deepfakes and misinformation are rife, it may be prudent to look for secondary data that has curation or assertion of provenance (e.g., through Web 3.0 style cryptographic signatures).

## AI Tools for Data Collection and Analysis: Your Digital Research Assistant

AI is like having a super-smart intern who works 24/7 and never asks for coffee breaks. AI can sift through social media faster than any human. Remember, while AI is powerful, it's just software - it is not infallible. Always apply your human insight to the results. Here's how it can help:

**Data scraping:** AI tools can gather data from websites faster than you can say "market analysis." The specific mechanism to extract data from particular websites is going to vary based on the specific AI tools you use. Some AI tools can also extract content from video clips and podcasts.

**Sentiment analysis:** Want to know what people *really* think about your product? AI tools can analyze the text of all your customers' review comments to extract what brings your customers joy (or drives them nuts!).

So there you have it, your guide to finding and using secondary data. It's like being a detective, but instead of solving crimes, you're solving business puzzles. Now go forth and data dive!

# Creating a Primary Data Collection Plan: Your Roadmap to Success

Now that you know where to find your market research gold, it's time to roll up your sleeves and get into the nitty-gritty of collecting and organizing that precious information. Don't worry; we'll make it as painless (and maybe even fun) as possible! Primary data collection involves obtaining original, firsthand information directly from the source for a specific research purpose, while secondary data collection uses existing information previously gathered by others. The primary difference lies in the origin and purpose of data collection. Primary data is newly collected for a specific research objective, while secondary data is repurposed from existing sources. Think of your data collection plan as a treasure map. It'll guide you to the information you need without getting lost in the sea of data out there.

## Passive (Organic) vs. Active Data Collection

**Passive Collection:** This is like setting up a net to catch fish. You're gathering data that's naturally occurring, such as website analytics or social media mentions, or if your everyday business processes (e.g., customer transactions) already collect the data you need. If you have existing operations collecting data, this can be a convenient place to start. Then, as you gain experience, you may decide to collect additional data as part of your everyday business processes to support your ongoing business performance monitoring needs, e.g., collecting customer satisfaction survey data after each transaction. If you have a website, set up Google Analytics on your website. It's free and gives you a wealth of information about your visitors!

**Active Collection:** This is more like going fishing with a rod. You're actively seeking out specific information through surveys, interviews, or focus groups. A quick poll on your social media can give you instant feedback from your audience.

## Creating Your Schedule

**Define your goals:** What do you want to learn?
**Choose your methods:** Surveys, analytics, or social listening?
**Set timelines:** When do you need this information?
**Assign responsibilities:** Who's doing what?

## Using Spreadsheets: Your Digital Filing Cabinet

Spreadsheets are like the Swiss Army knife of data organization. Create separate sheets for different data types (e.g., survey responses, website traffic, sales data). Use consistent naming conventions for your columns. Freeze the top row to keep your headers visible. Use filters to quickly sort and view specific data.

## Data Cleaning and Preprocessing: Polishing Your Digital Diamonds

Raw data is like a diamond in the rough - it needs some polishing to really shine. This typically includes:

**Remove duplicates**: No one likes seeing double!
**Fix formatting issues:** Make sure dates are dates, numbers are numbers, etc.
**Handle missing data:** Decide whether to remove or estimate missing values
**Standardize entries:** "USA" and "United States" should be the same thing in your data

For new data collection efforts, it is best to process the first few entries manually to understand the types of data defects that are prevalent and in need of cleanup. Once you know the data you are collecting better, you can automate the appropriate data cleanup actions if necessary.

# Surveys and Online Polls: Your Direct Line to Customer Insights

Surveys are your secret weapon for understanding customer perspectives. Think of them as a strategic conversation that transforms customer opinions into actionable business intelligence.

## Designing Your Survey Strategy

Successful surveys require thoughtful planning. Start by being specific about your market research objective - what specific insights are you seeking? Your goal might be understanding customer satisfaction and product preferences or identifying potential market opportunities. Audience selection is critical. Who are the most relevant respondents for your research? Consider demographics, psychographics, purchasing history, and engagement levels. Your target audience should directly align with your business' market research goals. For example, you may have an existing business process that collects customer satisfaction data. To focus on improving your customer satisfaction, you may need to focus on that customer who is unhappy to better understand why.

Survey length dramatically impacts completion rates. Aim for brevity - most respondents lose interest after 5-7 minutes. Prioritize essential questions and eliminate anything tangential to your core objectives. Mobile optimization isn't optional in today's smartphone-dominated world. Ensure your survey displays cleanly and functions smoothly across devices, particularly smartphones. Always pilot-test your survey with a small group. This reveals confusing questions and technical issues and helps refine your approach before broader distribution.

## Crafting Compelling Questions

Practical survey questions are clear, concise, and unbiased. Use straightforward language that avoids industry jargon. Steer clear of leading questions that suggest a preferred response. Mix question types strategically closed-ended questions generate quantitative data, and open-ended questions capture nuanced, qualitative insights. Start with easy, engaging questions to build respondent momentum.

## Response Formats That Illuminate Insights

Choose response formats that match your research goals.

**Likert** scales reveal sentiment intensity. The Likert scale is a popular rating system used in surveys to measure attitudes, opinions, and perceptions. Named after psychologist Rensis Likert, it typically offers respondents a range of options, usually from five to seven points, to express their level of agreement or disagreement with a given statement. Standard response options include "Strongly Disagree," "Disagree," "Neutral," "Agree," and "Strongly Agree." This structured format allows researchers to quantify subjective opinions, making it easier to analyze and compare data across different respondents and groups.

Multiple choice captures **categorical** preferences. Categorical preferences in surveys refer to the types of responses that can be grouped into distinct categories rather than measured on a numerical scale. These preferences typically involve questions that require respondents to select from predefined options, such as "What is your favorite color?" or "Which product do you prefer: A, B, or C?" Categorical data can be divided into two main types: nominal vs ordinal. Nominal data categorizes responses without implying any order (e.g., gender, brand preference), while ordinal data ranks responses in a specific order (e.g., satisfaction levels ranging from "very satisfied" to "very dissatisfied").

Rating scales measure **comparative** experiences. Comparative ratings in surveys allow respondents to evaluate and compare two or more items, products, or attributes simultaneously. This method is beneficial for understanding preferences, perceptions, and relative strengths among options. For example, a survey might ask participants to rate their satisfaction with two competing brands of smartphones by comparing features such as battery life, camera quality, and user interface.

**Open text fields** invite detailed feedback. Open text fields in surveys refer to questions that allow respondents to provide answers in their own words without being restricted to predefined options. These fields enable participants to express their thoughts, feelings, and opinions more freely, providing qualitative data that can offer deeper insights into their experiences and preferences. For example, an open text field might ask, "What do you think could improve our product?" This format encourages detailed feedback and can uncover valuable information that closed-ended questions may miss.

## Survey Tools and Technologies

Google Forms is an excellent tool for conducting market research surveys, offering a user-friendly platform to gather valuable insights from your customers. To get started, simply sign in with your Google account and create a new form. Begin by adding a clear title and description that outlines the purpose of your survey, ensuring respondents understand what you are asking them to contribute. Google Forms allows for easy customization, so feel free to incorporate themes and images that align with your brand to make the survey visually appealing. Once your survey is ready, share it via a link, email, or embed it on your website. After collecting responses, Google Forms provides built-in analytics tools that allow you to view summary statistics and visualize data through charts and graphs. For deeper analysis, you can export the data to Google Sheets for further exploration.

Chatbots are AI-powered conversational tools that interact with users through text or voice interfaces. They can provide an interactive, conversational survey experience that can increase engagement and response rates. They can ask questions, provide clarifications, and even probe for more detailed responses, mimicking a human interviewer.

## Maximizing Survey Participation

Incentivize participation thoughtfully. Offer meaningful rewards like discount codes, entry into prize draws, or exclusive content. Send gentle reminders, but avoid harassment. Take care to ensure that you:

Respect respondent time
Communicate survey purpose transparently.
Promise and deliver result summaries.
Make participation feel valuable.

Surveys are more than data collection - they're conversations that build customer relationships. Approach them as opportunities to demonstrate you value customer perspectives.

# Chapter 3: Working with Statistical Functions in Spreadsheets

## Market Research Problems Crying Out for Visualization

Remember when you were a kid and preferred picture books to plain text? Well, guess what - your brain still works that way! Data visualization takes your complex market research findings and transforms them into easily digestible visual stories. Imagine you've collected data on customer preferences for your new coffee shop. You could stare at rows of numbers, or you could create a vibrant pie chart showing the most popular flavors at a glance. Which sounds more appealing? In the table below are some common market research scenarios where visualization shines:

| Research Question | Data Collected | Chart Type | Decision Criteria |
|---|---|---|---|
| What is the market share distribution among competitors? | Sales data for each competitor in the market | Pie chart | The largest slice of the pie represents the market leader. |
| Which product features are most important to customers? | Customer ratings of importance for various product features | Horizontal bar chart | Features with the longest bars are considered most important to customers. |
| How do different age groups prefer various product categories? | Purchase data categorized by product type and customer age | Stacked bar chart | The largest stacked segments within each age group indicate preferred product categories. |
| How does product pricing compare to perceived value? | Customer ratings of product value at different price points | Bubble chart (x-y plot with bubble size) | Larger bubbles in the upper-right quadrant indicate optimal price-value combinations. |
| What is the distribution of customer lifetime value? | Calculated lifetime value for each customer | Histogram | A right-skewed distribution suggests a small number of high-value customers, while a normal distribution indicates more evenly spread customer value. |

| | | | |
|---|---|---|---|
| How do sales vary by region and product category? | Sales data categorized by geographic region and product type | Heat map | Darker colors or larger values in cells indicate stronger sales performance in specific region-product combinations. |
| How does customer sentiment vary across different product attributes? | Customer ratings on various product attributes | Radar chart | Larger areas in the chart indicate more positive sentiment, while smaller areas suggest areas for improvement |

Remember, the best visualization is the one that makes your audience say "Aha!" not "Huh?" Data visualization is your secret weapon for turning dry statistics into compelling stories. Even as a small business or solo entrepreneur, these data visualizations can be helpful not only in your decision-making but also persuasive for your customers and for business supporters (e.g., in obtaining financing)

# **Descriptive Statistics**

Ready to dive into the world of descriptive statistics? These descriptive statistics are the tools that help you summarize and make sense of your data. They provide a snapshot that helps guide deeper analysis and decision-making. By understanding how to calculate and interpret these descriptive statistics using spreadsheets, you'll be well-equipped to uncover valuable insights from your market research.

In general, using computed statistics rather than graphs or charts is preferable for several reasons. **Precision:** Statistics provide exact numerical values, offering more precise information than visual representations. **Objectivity:** Computed statistics reduce the risk of subjective interpretation that can occur with visual data. **Efficiency:** Statistics can quickly summarize large datasets, making it easier to compare across multiple variables or periods. **Quantitative analysis:** Statistics enable mathematical operations and further study, which is not always possible with visual representations. **Standardization:** Statistical measures provide a standardized way to compare different datasets or studies.

# Example: Market research problems requiring descriptive statistics

The table below illustrates several market research questions where descriptive statistics are typically used.

| Research Question | Data Collected | Statistic | Decision Criteria |
|---|---|---|---|
| What is the average customer spending per transaction? | Transaction amounts for all customers | Mean | A higher mean indicates greater average spending per transaction. |
| What is the most common product category purchased? | Purchase data categorized by product type | Mode | The category with the highest frequency is the most popular. |
| What is the typical time spent on the website by users? | Time spent on site for each user visit | Median | The median provides the central tendency of user engagement without being skewed by outliers. |
| How much variation exists in customer satisfaction scores? | Customer satisfaction ratings on a scale | Standard Deviation | A smaller standard deviation indicates more consistent satisfaction levels. |

| What is the average growth rate of sales over the past five years? | Annual sales figures for the last five years | Geometric Mean | A higher geometric mean indicates stronger consistent growth over time. |
|---|---|---|---|
| What is the distribution of customer ages? | Age data for all customers | Frequency Distribution | Peaks in the distribution reveal the most common age groups among customers. |
| How spread out are product prices across different categories? | Price data for all products | Range | A larger range indicates greater price diversity across the product lineup. |
| What percentage of customers are repeat buyers? | Purchase history data for all customers | Percentage | A higher percentage indicates stronger customer loyalty. |

## Defining, calculating, and interpreting descriptive statistics

The table below defines commonly used descriptive statistics and provides the respective Google Sheets formula for that statistic.

| Statistic | Definition | Formula | Element Definition | Sheets Formula |
|---|---|---|---|---|

| Term | Description | Formula | Variables | Excel |
|---|---|---|---|---|
| Mean ($\bar{x}$) | The average of a set of numbers | $\bar{x} = \dfrac{\sum_{i=1}^{n} x_i}{n}$ | $x_i$ = individual values<br>$n$ = number of values | =AVERAGE(range) |
| Median | The middle value in a sorted set of numbers | N/A (sorted position) | N/A | =MEDIAN(range) |
| Mode | The most frequently occurring value in a set | N/A (frequency count) | N/A | =MODE(range) |
| Geometric Mean (GM) | The nth root of the product of n numbers | $GM = \sqrt[n]{x_1 \times x_2 \times \ldots \times x_n}$ alternatively $GM = \sqrt[n]{\prod_{i=1}^{n} x_i}$ | $x_i$ = individual values<br>$n$ = number of values | =GEOMEAN(range) |
| Range (R) | The difference between the largest and smallest values | $R = x_{max} - x_{min}$ | $x_{max}$ = maximum value<br>$x_{min}$ = minimum value | =MAX(range)<br>MIN(range) |
| Percentage | A proportion expressed as a fraction of 100 | $P = \dfrac{x}{n} \times 100\%$ | $x$ = part<br>$n$ = whole | =(x/n)*100 |

| | | | | |
|---|---|---|---|---|
| Frequency Distribution | A summary of how often each value occurs in a dataset | N/A (count of occurrences) | N/A | =FREQUENCY(data, bins) |
| Standard Deviation ($\sigma$) | A measure of variability or dispersion from the mean | $\sigma = \sqrt{\frac{\sum_{i=1}^{n}(x_i - \bar{x})^2}{n-1}}$ | $x_i$ = individual values<br>$\bar{x}$ = mean<br>$n$ = number of values | =STDEV.S(range) |

# Inferential Statistics and Hypothesis Testing

Ready to take your market research skills to the next level? Let's dive into the fascinating world of inferential statistics and hypothesis testing. Don't worry if these terms sound intimidating - we'll break them down into friendly, spreadsheet-ready concepts.

### What is an Inference?

Before we jump in, let's clarify what we mean by an "inference." An inference is a conclusion drawn from evidence and reasoning (e.g., using hypothesis testing). Statistics is using data from a sample to draw conclusions about a larger population. It's like tasting a spoonful of soup and deciding if the whole pot needs more salt!

You may also hear the term Inference used in the context of AI tools and processes. "AI inference" refers to the process of using a trained machine learning model to make predictions or decisions on new, unseen data. After an AI model has been trained on a dataset, it can take new inputs and produce outputs based on the patterns it learned during training. For instance, a trained image recognition model can "infer" the contents of new images that haven't been seen before. There are some key differences between AI and statistical inferences:

**Purpose:** Statistical inference aims to understand *population characteristics*, while AI inference focuses on making *predictions or classifications*.

**Methodology:** Statistical inference relies on probability theory and hypothesis testing, whereas AI inference uses trained models and algorithms.

**Scope:** Statistical inference *generalizes* from samples to populations, while AI inference *applies learned patterns* to individual cases.

**Interpretability:** Statistical models often *prioritize interpretability and understanding* relationships between variables, while many AI models (like deep neural networks) may *sacrifice interpretability for predictive power*.

Both types of inference are valuable in data analysis. Statistical inference provides insights into underlying processes and AI inference excels at pattern recognition and prediction tasks.

## Inferential Statistics: The Big Picture

Inferential statistics is all about making educated guesses about a larger group based on a small sample. It's like being a detective who examines a few clues to solve a bigger mystery. These techniques help us estimate population parameters from sample statistics, test hypotheses about populations, and predict future outcomes based on past data.

## Hypothesis Testing: Your Statistical Crystal Ball

Hypothesis testing is a formal process for investigating our ideas about the world using data. Here's how it works:

Form a hypothesis (e.g., "Our new marketing campaign will increase sales")

Collect data (e.g., sales data before, during, and after the marketing campaign)

Use statistical tests to see if your data supports your hypothesis

# Market research problems requiring these inferential statistics

The table below illustrates several market research questions where inferential statistics are typically used. Recall that inferential statistics is all about drawing conclusions and making predictions. I should note that conclusions and predictions can also be made using some forms of visualization.

| Research Question | Data Collected | Chart Type | Decision Criteria |
|---|---|---|---|
| How has customer satisfaction changed over time? | Customer satisfaction scores over multiple time periods | Line chart | An upward trend indicates improving satisfaction, while a downward trend suggests declining satisfaction. |
| What is the trend in market growth rate over time? | Year-over-year market size data | Semi-log line chart (y-axis logarithmic) | A straight line indicates consistent percentage growth, while curves suggest accelerating or decelerating growth rates. |
| Is there a significant difference in product satisfaction between male and female customers? | Customer satisfaction scores and gender data | Independent samples t-test | If p-value < 0.05, conclude there is a significant difference in satisfaction between genders. |
| Does a new marketing campaign increase brand awareness compared to the old campaign? | Brand awareness scores before and after the new campaign | Paired samples t-test | If p-value < 0.05, conclude the new campaign significantly increases brand awareness. |

| | | | | |
|---|---|---|---|---|
| Are there significant differences in customer preferences across different age groups? | Customer preference ratings and age group data | Chi-square test of independence | If p-value < 0.05, conclude there are significant differences in preferences across age groups. |
| Is there a significant difference in website conversion rates between desktop and mobile users? | Conversion rates for desktop and mobile users | Z-test for proportions | If p-value < 0.05, conclude there is a significant difference in conversion rates between platforms. |
| Do different pricing strategies affect sales volume across multiple store locations? | Sales data from stores using different pricing strategies | One-way ANOVA | If F-statistic is significant (p < 0.05), conclude pricing strategies have a significant effect on sales volume. |

## Defining, calculating, and interpreting inferential statistics

The table below defines commonly used inferential statistics and provides the respective Google Sheets formula for that statistic.

| Statistic | Definition | Formula | Element Definitions | Sheets Formula |
|---|---|---|---|---|

| Test | Description | Formula | Variables | Excel Function |
|---|---|---|---|---|
| t-test (independent samples) | Compares the means of two independent groups to determine if they are significantly different | $t = (\bar{x}_1 - \bar{x}_2) / \sqrt{(\sigma_1^2/n_1) + (\sigma_2^2/n_2)}$ | $\bar{x}_1, \bar{x}_2$: means of groups 1 and 2; $\sigma_1^2, \sigma_2^2$: variances of groups 1 and 2; $n_1, n_2$: sample sizes of groups 1 and 2 | =T.TEST(range1, range2, 2, 2) |
| t-test (paired samples) | Compares the means of two related groups to determine if they are significantly different | $t = \bar{d} / (\sigma / \sqrt{n})$ | $\bar{d}$: mean difference between paired observations; $\sigma$: standard deviation of differences; n: number of pairs | =T.TEST(range1, range2, 2, 1) |
| Chi-Square test | Tests the independence of two categorical variables | $\chi^2 = \Sigma((O - E)^2 / E)$ | O: observed frequency; E: expected frequency | =CHISQ.TEST(actual_range, expected_range) |
| Z-test | Compares a sample mean to a known population mean | $z = (\bar{x} - \mu) / (\sigma / \sqrt{n})$ | $\bar{x}$: sample mean; $\mu$: population mean; $\sigma$: population standard deviation; n: sample size | No built-in function; use =NORM.S.DIST() for p-value |

| | | | | |
|---|---|---|---|---|
| F-Test | Compares the variances of two populations | $F = \sigma_1^2 / \sigma_2^2$ | $\sigma_1^2$, $\sigma_2^2$: variances of populations 1 and 2 | |
| One Way ANOVA | Compares means of three or more groups | F = (Between Group Variability) / (Within Group Variability) | Between Group Variability: variance between group means Within Group Variability: average variance within groups | =F.TEST(array1, array2, ..., arrayn) |

## F-tests and ANOVA: Comparing Groups Like a Pro

F-tests and ANOVA (Analysis of Variance) help us compare groups to see if they're significantly different from each other. The F-test and one-way ANOVA are closely related statistical methods used to assess the equality of means across multiple groups. Both rely on the F-statistic, which is a ratio of variances that measures the variability between group means compared to the variability within groups. In a one-way ANOVA, the F-test is employed to determine if there are any statistically significant differences among the means of three or more independent groups. The F-statistic is calculated as the ratio of between-group variance (explained variance) to within-group variance (unexplained variance). If the calculated F-value is larger than the critical value from the F-distribution, it suggests that the differences in group means are unlikely to be due to random chance alone, leading to the rejection of the null hypothesis that all group means are equal. This makes the F-test a fundamental component of ANOVA, providing a framework for evaluating whether observed differences in data are meaningful or merely due to variability within groups. For ANOVA in Google Sheets, you can use add-ons like XLMiner Analysis ToolPak.

### Interpreting Results: Decoding the Numbers

After running your tests, you'll get a p-value. This tells you the probability of getting your results if your hypothesis were false. Generally:
If $p < 0.05$, your results are statistically significant
If $p \geq 0.05$, your results are not statistically significant
Remember, "statistically significant" doesn't always mean "important in real life." Use your business sense along with these statistical tools! Even the best data detectives can make mistakes. Here are two common errors to watch out for:

**Type I Error:** Concluding there's an effect when there isn't (**false positive**)

**Type II Error:** Missing an effect that actually exists (**false negative**)

To minimize these errors: Use an appropriate significance level (usually 0.05), ensure your sample size is large enough, and be cautious about making strong claims based on borderline results

Inferential statistics and hypothesis testing are powerful tools for the use of data in decision-making. They help you go beyond just describing your data to making educated predictions and comparisons. Remember, these are tools that are here to support your decision-making, not replace it. Combine your statistical insights with your business acumen, and you'll be making smarter, data-backed decisions in no time! Now go forth and infer, hypothesize, and analyze! Your data is waiting to tell its story, and you're now equipped to listen and draw meaningful conclusions.

# Correlation and Regression Analysis

Hey there, data detective! Ready to explore the fascinating world of correlation and regression analysis? These powerful tools can help you uncover hidden relationships in your market research data. Don't worry if these terms sound a bit intimidating - we'll break them down into bite-sized, spreadsheet-friendly pieces.

# Example: Market research problems requiring these types of statistics

The table below illustrates several market research questions where correlation and regression statistics are typically used. Correlation and regression can also be inspected using some forms of visualization.

| Research Question | Data Collected | Chart Type | Decision Criteria |
|---|---|---|---|
| What is the correlation between advertising spend and sales revenue? | Monthly advertising expenditure and corresponding sales revenue | Scatter plot (x-y plot) | A strong positive correlation suggests advertising effectiveness, while a weak or negative correlation may indicate inefficient spending. |
| Is there a relationship between customer satisfaction and the number of customer service interactions? | Customer satisfaction scores and number of service interactions | Spearman's rank correlation | If rho ≠ 0 and $p < 0.05$, conclude there is a significant relationship between satisfaction and service interactions. |

| Is there a correlation between advertising spend and revenue growth? | Monthly advertising expenditure and corresponding revenue data | Pearson correlation coefficient | If r > 0.5 and p < 0.05, conclude there is a significant positive correlation between ad spend and revenue growth. |
|---|---|---|---|

## Defining, calculating, and interpreting inferential statistics

Imagine you're trying to figure out if there's a connection between how much you spend on advertising and your monthly sales. That's where correlation and regression come in handy!

**Correlation** tells you if there's a relationship between two variables and how strong that relationship is. It provides some measure of the strength of that relationship but does not provide any indication of the direction of influence in the relationship. The correlation coefficient (usually represented as 'r') ranges from -1 to 1:

    1 means a perfect positive correlation (as one goes up, the other goes up)

    -1 means a perfect negative correlation (as one goes up, the other goes down)

    0 means no correlation (they don't seem to be related)

**Regression** goes a step further, helping you predict one variable based on another. Most commonly, regression assumes a linear relationship between the variables. Visually, you can interpret this as a scatter plot of the data pairs with a line fitted through the scatter plot such that the aggregate error distance between the line and scattered points is minimized. The process can also be generalized to fit the data to other curves, e.g., exponentials, logistic curves, etc.

**Causation** establishes that changes in one variable directly result in changes in another variable. While correlation and regression can suggest a potential causal relationship, they alone are insufficient to prove causation. Additional criteria must be met in order to establish causation, such as *temporal precedence* (the cause must precede the effect), the *absence of alternative explanations*, and, ideally, experimental evidence where *other factors are controlled*. It's crucial to remember the adage, **"correlation does not imply causation."** Many correlated variables may be influenced by unseen factors or mere coincidence rather than a direct causal link. Just because two things are correlated doesn't mean one causes the other. Ice cream sales and sunburn cases might be correlated, but eating ice cream doesn't cause sunburn!

Even seasoned data analysts can make mistakes. Here are some pitfalls to watch out for:

**Extrapolating beyond your data:** Be cautious about using your regression model to predict far beyond the range of your data.

**Ignoring other variables:** There might be other factors influencing your dependent variable that you still need to consider.

**Assuming linearity:** Not all relationships are linear. Sometimes, you might need more advanced techniques like non-linear regression.

The table below defines commonly used inferential statistics and provides the respective Google Sheets formula for that statistic.

| Regression Statistic | Definition | Formula | Element Definitions | Sheets Formula |
|---|---|---|---|---|
| Correlation (r) | Measures the strength and direction of a linear relationship between two variables | $r = \Sigma((x - \bar{x})(y - \bar{\square})) / \sqrt{(\Sigma(x - \bar{x})^2 \Sigma(y - \bar{\square})^2)}$ | x, y: individual values  $\bar{x}, \bar{\square}$: means of x and y | =CORREL( range1, range2) |
| Regression | Predicts the value of a dependent | $y = mx + b$ | y: dependent variable | =FORECAST(x, |

| | | | | |
|---|---|---|---|---|
| | variable based on the value of an independent variable | | x: independent variable<br>m: slope<br>b: y-intercept | known_y's, known_x's) |
| Spearman's Rank Correlation | Measures the strength and direction of association between two ranked variables | $\rho = 1 - (6 \Sigma d^2 / (n(n^2 - 1)))$ | d: difference between ranks<br>n: number of observations | No built-in function; use =CORREL( ) on ranked data |
| Pearson's Correlation Coefficient | Measures the strength and direction of linear relationship between two variables | $r = \Sigma((x - \bar{x})(y - \Box)) / \sqrt{(\Sigma(x - \bar{x})^2 \Sigma(y - \Box)^2)}$ | x, y: individual values<br>$\bar{x}$, $\Box$: means of x and y | =CORREL( range1, range2) |

Correlation and regression analysis are potent tools in your market research toolkit. They can help you uncover relationships in your data and make predictions about future trends. Remember, these tools are here to support your decision-making, not replace it. Always combine your statistical insights with your business acumen and common sense. Now, go forth and analyze! Your data is full of hidden connections waiting to be discovered.

# Supercharging Your Market Research: Heuristics & AI Predictive Techniques:

Ready to add some extra oomph to your market research toolkit? Let's dive into the world of heuristics and AI predictive techniques. Don't worry if these sound like terms from a sci-fi movie - we'll break them down into practical, easy-to-understand concepts that can really boost your market research game.

Heuristics are like mental shortcuts or rules of thumb that help us make quick decisions without overthinking. They're the gut feelings and educated guesses that often guide our choices.

## Heuristics in Market Research

In market research, heuristics can be incredibly useful. They help you make quick assessments and decisions when you need more data or time for in-depth analysis. Here are some common heuristics used in market research:

**Availability Heuristic:** This is when we make judgments based on how easily we can recall examples. For instance, you might assume a product is popular because you've seen a lot of ads for it recently.

**Representativeness Heuristic:** This involves making judgments based on how similar something is to a typical case. For example, you might assume a customer who fits your typical buyer profile will have similar preferences.

**Anchoring Heuristic:** This is when we rely heavily on the first piece of information we receive. In pricing research, a customer's first price can significantly influence their perception of value.

**Peak-End Rule:** People tend to judge an experience based on its peak (most intense point) and/or its end, rather than the average of the entire experience. This can be crucial in interpreting customer satisfaction surveys.

While heuristics can be powerful tools, using them cautiously is important. The key is to use heuristics as a starting point, but always be ready to adjust your thinking based on new data or insights.

## AI Market Research: Practical Applications

Now, let's talk about how AI is revolutionizing market research predictions. It's like having a super-smart assistant who can crunch numbers and spot patterns faster than any human. Some example use cases include:

**Demand Forecasting:** By analyzing historical sales data, market trends, and even factors like weather, AI can predict future demand for your products or services.

**Trend Prediction:** By analyzing vast amounts of online data, AI can spot emerging trends before they hit the mainstream, giving you a competitive edge.

You don't need to be a tech wizard to start using AI in your market research. Many user-friendly tools and platforms offer AI-powered analytics: Google Analytics uses AI to provide insights about your website visitors. Social media management tools often include AI-powered sentiment analysis. Many survey platforms now offer AI-assisted analysis of open-ended responses.

Remember, AI is just a software tool, not a replacement for your business acumen. The most powerful approach combines AI's data-crunching abilities with your industry knowledge and intuition. Heuristics and AI predictive techniques are powerful additions to your market research toolkit. Heuristics help you make quick, intuitive decisions, while AI can process vast amounts of data to uncover insights and predict trends. Combining these approaches with traditional research methods, you'll be well-equipped to navigate the complex world of market research. You'll make faster decisions with heuristics, uncover deeper insights with AI, and always stay one step ahead of the competition. So go forth and explore!

# Chapter 4: Applying Market Research Insights to Grow Your Business

## Identifying Market Opportunities and Trends: Your Roadmap to Success

Hey there, business trailblazer! Ready to turn those market research insights into real growth for your business? Let's dive into identifying market opportunities and trends and learn how to use this information to create a killer value proposition. Buckle up—it's time to take your business to the next level!

### Spotting Your Perfect Customer: Identifying Target Audience Segments and Personas

Remember when you were a kid and played "Where's Waldo?" Finding your ideal customer is a bit like that, but way more fun (and profitable)! Here's how to do it:

**Slice and Dice Your Data:** Look at your market research data and start grouping customers based on shared characteristics. These could be demographics (age, location, income), psychographics (values, interests, lifestyles), or behaviors (buying habits, brand loyalty).

**Create Your Segments:** Once you've identified these groups, give each segment a name so that you can conveniently refer to them when targeting them in your business plans.

**Develop Personas:** Now, let's bring these segments to life! Create fictional characters that typify each segment. Give them names, backstories, goals, and challenges, so that you can easily explain the value proposition they need to see to use your product. For instance, "Emily, the 28-year-old marketing executive who values sustainability and convenience."

**Prioritize Your Segments:** Not all segments are created equal. Identify the segments that offer the most potential for your business based on factors like size, growth potential, and alignment with your offerings.

Don't just rely on data—talk to real customers! Their stories and feedback can add depth to your personas and uncover insights you might have missed.

## Standing Out from the Crowd: Creating a Unique Value Proposition and Positioning Statement

Now that you know your ideal customers, it's time to tell them why they should choose you over the competition. This is where your unique value proposition (UVP) and positioning statement come in. Your UVP is like your business's superhero catchphrase—it should be clear, compelling, and memorable. Here's how to create one: **Identify Your Customers' Pain Points:** What problems or needs did your market research uncover? **Highlight Your Solution:** How does your product or service address these pain points? **Showcase Your Unique Angle:** What makes your solution different or better than alternatives? **Keep It Simple:** Aim for a clear, concise statement that a 10-year-old could understand. **Example UVP:** "We deliver farm-fresh, organic produce to your doorstep in under 2 hours, so you can enjoy healthy meals without the hassle of grocery shopping."

### Nailing Your Positioning Statement

Your positioning statement is like a more detailed version of your UVP. It should clearly define:

**Who you serve:** Your target audience
**What you offer:** Your product or service category
**How you're different:** Your unique benefits
**Why customers should believe you:** Your proof or credibility

Here's a template to get you started:

"For [target audience], [your brand] is the [product/service category] that [key benefit] because [reason to believe]."

Example: "For busy urban professionals, Green Basket is the organic produce delivery service that provides the freshest, locally sourced vegetables and fruits because we partner directly with local farmers and guarantee delivery within 2 hours of harvest."

Remember, your UVP and positioning statement aren't set in stone. As market trends change and your business evolves, feel free to revisit and refine them. You're turning your market research into actionable strategies by identifying your target audience segments, creating detailed personas, and crafting a compelling UVP and positioning statement. You're not just gathering data—you're using it to speak directly to your ideal customers and show them why your business is the perfect fit for their needs.

So go ahead and put these insights into action! Your perfectly positioned business is ready to capture those market opportunities and ride the trends to success. You've got this!

Evaluating Business Ideas and Developing a Business Strategy

Now that you've identified your target audience and crafted your unique value proposition, it's time to put those insights into action. Let's dive into developing a killer marketing mix and tactics that'll make your business shine!

# Developing a Marketing Mix and Tactics: Your Recipe for Success

Think of your marketing mix as a delicious business smoothie. You need the right ingredients in the right proportions to create something irresistible. Here's how to blend your perfect marketing mix using the classic 4 Ps:

**Product:** What are you offering? Use your market research to refine your product or service to meet your target audience's needs. Consider offering different versions or packages to appeal to different segments.

**Price:** How much will you charge? Your research should give you insights into what your customers are willing to pay. Don't just focus on being the cheapest. Sometimes, a higher price can position you as a premium option.

**Place:** Where will you sell? This could be a physical location, online, or both. Make sure your distribution channels align with where your target audience likes to shop.

**Promotion:** How will you spread the word? This includes advertising, social media, content marketing, and more. Choose promotional channels that resonate with your target audience. If your research shows they love Instagram, that's where you need to be!

visual elements that reflect the data from your main sheets; use the "Insert" menu to add charts like line graphs or tables. To link data dynamically, utilize functions such as IMPORTRANGE to pull in data from other sheets or QUERY to filter and refine the information displayed. Enhance interactivity by adding slicers or filters, allowing users to customize the view based on specific criteria. Finally, regularly update your dashboard by ensuring that any changes in the source sheets are reflected automatically, providing real-time insights into your business metrics.

## Adjusting and Refining Marketing Strategies Based on Data

Now that you're tracking your performance, it's time to put that data to work. Here's how to stay agile and keep improving:
**Regular Review Sessions:** Set aside time each month or quarter to review your metrics and discuss what's working and what's not.
**A/B Testing:** Experiment with different versions of your marketing materials to see what resonates best with your audience.
**Customer Feedback Loops:** Regularly ask for and act on customer feedback. They're your best source of insights!
**Competitor Analysis:** Keep an eye on what your competitors are doing. Can you learn from their successes or failures?
**Trend Watching:** Stay updated on industry trends and be ready to pivot if needed.
**Continuous Learning:** Invest in ongoing market research to keep your finger on the pulse of your audience's evolving needs.

Adjusting your strategy isn't a sign of failure – it's a sign of responsive business management. Be proud of your ability to adapt! By creating a solid marketing mix, implementing targeted tactics, and consistently monitoring and adjusting your approach, your business is up for long-term success.

Remember, market research isn't a one-and-done deal. It's an ongoing process that helps you stay connected with your customers and ahead of the competition. So keep asking questions, keep analyzing data, and keep refining your strategies. Your business will thank you for it! Now, go out there and show the world what your business can do. You've got the tools, the knowledge, and the drive to succeed. The market is waiting for you!

# Conclusion: Your Journey Through Market Research Math

Congratulations on reaching the end of this book! We've explored the essential concepts and tools of market research math that can empower your small business to thrive. We began by understanding the importance of market research and how it informs decision-making. You learned to identify market opportunities and trends, develop effective marketing strategies, and apply statistical functions using spreadsheets to analyze data. We delved into descriptive and inferential statistics and the power of correlation and regression analysis in uncovering data relationships. Finally, we discussed how to create actionable insights from your research to drive growth and success.

I want to extend my heartfelt thanks for taking the time to read this book. Your commitment to enhancing your market research skills will undoubtedly benefit your business. If you found this book helpful, please take a moment to leave a review on Amazon. Your feedback not only helps me improve future editions but also assists other readers in discovering valuable resources for their own market research journeys.

Thank you once again for being a part of this exploration. I wish you all the best as you apply these insights to grow your business and achieve your goals!

# Glossary

Here's a table summarizing the definitions and examples of when to use various statistics in market research:

| Statistic | Definition | Example Use |
|---|---|---|
| Chi-Square Test | A statistical test used to determine whether there is a significant association between two categorical variables. | A retailer analyzes customer survey data to see if there is a relationship between gender and product preference. |
| Correlation (r) | A measure of the strength and direction of the linear relationship between two variables. | A marketer examines the relationship between social media engagement and website traffic to assess marketing effectiveness. |
| F-Test | A statistical test used to compare the variances of two populations to see if they are significantly different. | A quality control manager compares the variability in product dimensions from two different production methods. |
| Frequency Distribution | A summary of how often each value occurs in a dataset, often displayed in a table or graph. | A business analyzes customer feedback ratings to visualize how frequently each rating (e.g., 1-5 stars) is given. |

## Market Research Math for Small Business

| | | |
|---|---|---|
| Geometric Mean (GM) | The average of a set of products calculated by multiplying all the values together and taking the nth root, where n is the number of values. | A financial analyst uses the geometric mean to calculate average growth rates for investment returns over multiple years. |
| Inference | The process of drawing conclusions about a population based on sample data. | A researcher uses sample survey results to make predictions about customer behavior in the entire market. |
| Mean (x) | The average value of a dataset, calculated by summing all values and dividing by the number of values. | A company calculates the average purchase amount per customer to assess overall spending behavior. |
| Median | The middle value in a dataset when arranged in ascending order, which divides the data into two equal halves. | A business evaluates median income levels among customers to identify target demographics for marketing efforts. |
| Mode | The value that appears most frequently in a dataset. | A product manager identifies the most common customer complaint from survey responses to prioritize improvements. |
| One Way ANOVA | A statistical test used to compare means among three or more groups to determine if at least one group mean is significantly different from others. | A company tests three different advertising strategies across various regions to see which leads to higher sales performance. |

| | | |
|---|---|---|
| Pearson's Correlation Coefficient | A measure of the linear correlation between two variables, giving a value between -1 and 1. | An analyst studies the relationship between customer satisfaction scores and repeat purchase rates to understand loyalty trends. |
| Percentage | A way of expressing a number as a fraction of 100, often used to compare proportions within datasets. | A marketer calculates the percentage of customers who prefer online shopping versus in-store shopping based on survey results. |
| Range (R) | The difference between the highest and lowest values in a dataset, indicating variability. | A business analyzes the range of sales figures over several months to understand fluctuations in performance. |
| Regression | A statistical method for modeling the relationship between a dependent variable and one or more independent variables to predict outcomes. | A company uses regression analysis to predict future sales based on historical advertising spend and economic indicators. |
| Spearman's Rank Correlation | A non-parametric measure that assesses the strength and direction of association between two ranked variables. | A researcher examines whether higher customer ratings correlate with increased likelihood of recommending a product. |
| Standard Deviation ($\sigma$) | A measure of the amount of variation or dispersion in a set of values, indicating how spread out the values are around the mean. | An analyst calculates standard deviation for customer satisfaction scores to assess consistency in service delivery. |

Now, let's talk tactics. These are the specific actions you'll take to implement your marketing mix: **Content Marketing:** Create content that addresses your audience's pain points to demonstrate your product's value proposition. **Social Media Engagement:** Build relationships with your audience on their preferred platforms. **Email Marketing:** Nurture leads and keep customers engaged with **personalized communications.** **Influencer Partnerships:** Collaborate with influencers who resonate with your target audience. **Customer Loyalty Programs:** Encourage repeat business and word-of-mouth referrals.

Remember, your tactics should always tie back to your overall strategy and be informed by your market research. Don't just do something because it's trendy – do it because your research shows it'll work for your audience!

# Continuously Monitoring and Adjusting Business Strategies

Alright, strategy superstar! Your plan is in place, but the work continues beyond there. The market is constantly changing, and so should your strategies. Let's look at how to stay on top of your game. You can't improve what you don't measure. Here are some key metrics to keep an eye on:

**Sales Revenue:** The most obvious but always important!
**Customer Acquisition Cost (CAC):** How much does it cost to get a new customer?
**Customer Lifetime Value (CLV):** How much is a customer worth to you over time?
**Conversion Rate:** What percentage of leads become customers?
Customer Satisfaction Score (CSAT): How happy are your customers?
Net Promoter Score (NPS): How likely are customers to recommend you?
**Market Share:** What portion of the total market are you capturing?

Set up a dashboard to track these metrics regularly. Many CRM and analytics tools can help automate this process. Still, this can be done relatively quickly for a small business using Google Sheets. After organizing your data in Google Sheets, ensure each column has a clear title and includes relevant numerical values and dates. Create a new sheet specifically for your dashboard, where you can insert various charts and

| | | |
|---|---|---|
| t-test (independent samples) | A statistical test used to compare the means of two independent groups to determine if they are significantly different. | A company compares average satisfaction scores between users of two different software versions to see which performs better. |
| t-test (paired samples) | A statistical test used to compare means from the same group at different times or under different conditions. | A restaurant evaluates customer satisfaction before and after implementing a new menu item to see if there is a significant improvement. |
| Z-test | A statistical test used to determine whether there is a significant difference between sample and population means when the population variance is known. | An analyst tests whether average sales during a promotional period differ significantly from typical sales figures based on historical data. |

# Resources

Below is a curated list of books for further learning that will encourage entrepreneurs to continue developing their market research skills beyond the book, fostering ongoing growth and improvement.

## Marketing

Pride, W.M & Ferrell, O.C. (1983) *Marketing: Basic Concepts and Definitions*, Houghton Mifflin Co, Boston, MA

Assael, H. (1985) *Marketing Management: Strategy and Action*, Kent Publishing Co., Boston, MA

Terpstra, V. (1987) *International Marketing*, The Dryden Press, New York, NY

## Visualization

Tufte, E.R., (1983) *The Visual Display of Quantitative Information*, Graphics Press, Cheshire, CT.

Tufte, E.R., (1990) *Envisioning Information*, Graphics Press, Cheshire, CT.

Tufte, E.R., (1997) Visual Explanations: Images and Quantities, Evidence and Narrative, Graphics Press, Cheshire, CT.

Tufte, E.R., (2006) *Beautiful Evidence*, Graphics Press, Cheshire, CT.

## Statistics

Dunn, P.K. (2021) Scientific Research and Methodology, available online at: https://bookdown.org/pkaldunn/Book/

Davis, D. & Cosenza, R.M. (1985) Business Research for Decisionmaking, Kent Publishing Company, Boston, MA.

## Surveys

Jarrett, C & Krug, S. (2021) Surveys That Work: A Practical Guide for Designing and Running Better Surveys, Rosenfeld Media

Levesque, R, (2019) Ask: The Counterintuitive Online Method to Discover Exactly What Your Customers Want to Buy . . . Create a Mass of Raving Fans . . . and Take Any Business to the Next Level, Hay House Business

# Google Apps

Roberts, B. (2016) Google Sheet Functions: A step-by-step guide (Google Workspace apps) ASIN : B01NBHMZI9

Roberts, B (2021) Beginner's Guide to Google Drive (Google Workspace apps) ASIN : B08X9XX6ZR

Roberts, B. (2016) Beginner's Guide to Google Docs (Google Workspace apps) ASIN : B01EXS6AYE

Roberts, B. (2021) Step-by-step Guide to Google Forms (Google Workspace apps) ASIN : B08XXPQMLJ

## Please Leave a Review Comment!

Thank you for taking the time to explore this non-fiction work. If you found the insights valuable, we invite you to scan the QR code below and share your thoughts in a review. Your feedback is crucial in helping others navigate this important subject By sharing your honest perspective, you empower fellow readers and support our ongoing efforts to cultivate a knowledgeable community. We appreciate your engagement and dedication to enhancing technology ethics for everyone!

## About the Author

Thank you for diving into this book! We invite you to scan the QR code below to learn more about the author and follow his work. By doing so, you'll gain access to valuable insights and updates on future projects, fostering a deeper connection to the themes explored in these pages. Additionally, your engagement helps build a community of readers committed to understanding and addressing the challenges in this field. We genuinely appreciate your time and support, and we hope you find even greater enjoyment in the author's next book!

www.ingramcontent.com/pod-product-compliance
Lightning Source LLC
Chambersburg PA
CBHW070939220526
45469CB00007B/2449